Beneath a Sky of Silver Suns

Under skies with twinkling rays,
Mice do break into ballet.
Swaying tails and little feet,
Pigeons join, they can't be beat.

The sunbeams tickle leaves above,
Bouncing beats that push and shove.
Frogs in hats sing funny tunes,
While turtles groove with silly swoons.

Every cloud has giggles stored,
With every breeze, the laughter soared.
As daisies swirl in cheeky cheer,
A parade of joy draws near.

So cast away your cares today,
Join this dance without delay.
Under sunlight's silver glimmer,
Life's joy feels more like a shimmer.

The Gathering of the Fragrant Wild

In a meadow wide and bright,
Flowers gossip, what a sight!
Daisies chat with roses fair,
While bees buzz tunes that fill the air.

Tall sunflowers on fashion's quest,
Strutting high in golden vest.
Butterflies wear polka dots,
Taking flight, they spin in plots.

A picnic spread with veggies bold,
Radishes in dresses gold.
The ants bring snacks, a splendid feast,
As squirrels break into a feast.

So gather 'round this fragrant scene,
Where nature's jesters like to glean.
With wild delights, the laughter swells,
In nature's bowl, joy surely dwells.

Sylvan Serenade of the Soul

In the glades where gnomes reside,
Bubbles rise as giggles glide.
Each tree hums a jolly tune,
To the light of a grinning moon.

With rabbits tap dancing on logs,
And foxes prancing like silly dogs.
The brook giggles with crystal glee,
As fish wear crowns and swim carefree.

Frogs compose a symphony,
While toads leap in jubilee.
A raucous band of twany sprites,
Stir up laughter every night.

So come, dear friend, to this delight,
Where fun and laughter take their flight.
With every leaf a joyous cheer,
In sylvan tunes, we find our dear.

Roots in Reverie

Beneath the soil, a story swirls,
A gopher's laugh, in tangled whirls.
With each small bump, a poke and cheer,
The roots are dancing, have no fear.

A squirrel scolds a wayward friend,
"Your acorn stash is not the end!"
While daisies giggle, swaying wide,
In this secret world, we all abide.

Vita Beneath the Boughs

The branches sway with whispers sweet,
As birds play tag, their nimble feet.
A chipmunk slides upon a leaf,
Claiming it's his, in comical grief.

The shadows dance in sunlight's grace,
A patchwork quilt in nature's space.
And laughter flows like streams of light,
In this grand party, pure delight.

Allure of the Alleys

In narrow lanes where secrets thrive,
A cat named Whiskers does a dive.
Among the weeds, he claims his throne,
As pigeons plot to steal his bone.

The laughter echoes, playful tone,
A treasure hunt for cheese and scone.
With every turn, a jest unfolds,
In alleys where the magic's bold.

The Crescendo of Canopies

The leaves are clapping, what a show!
As breezes hum, they steal the glow.
A raccoon wears a leafy crown,
While drumming squirrels won't back down.

In the canopies, a tale is spun,
Of acorn parties, oh what fun!
With moonlight glinting, stars in tow,
The woods an orchestra, in full flow.

Harmony of the Hidden

In the thicket, a squirrel did prance,
With acorns dancing, he led his own dance.
A crow overhead cawed a loud tune,
While a raccoon sighed, 'I'll be home soon.'

The flowers giggled as rabbits leapt,
In secret meetings where no one slept.
A butterfly whispered a joke to a bee,
'Why did you buzz? It's too sweet for me!'

The Lull of the Woodland

The trees hummed softly, a slumbering beat,
A fox in a tuxedo thought it quite sweet.
He tipped his hat to a drowsy old owl,
Who nodded back with a dignified scowl.

The mushrooms chuckled, their colors so bright,
As the sun peeked in, painting all with light.
A snail on his journey, oh so slow,
Muttered, 'Time's just a myth, don't you know?'

Footsteps in Ferns

Through ferns that swayed in rhythm and rhyme,
A hedgehog rolled by, pretending it's prime.
He tripped on a stone, gave a little yelp,
As a rabbit exclaimed, 'Did you need some help?'

Whispers of laughter erupted from leaves,
As ants on a mission plotted their thieves.
A ladybug winked, 'Listen here, chap,'
'We've got the best beans for a forest rap!'

Original title:
Juniper Joys

Copyright © 2025 Creative Arts Management OÜ
All rights reserved.

Author: Arabella Whitmore
ISBN HARDBACK: 978-1-80566-740-7
ISBN PAPERBACK: 978-1-80566-869-5

Enchanted Forest Dreams

In the woods where badgers play,
Squirrels gossip all the day.
Fairy hats on every tree,
Wobbling mushrooms dance for free.

Elves bake pies with sprightly glee,
Mixing winks in every spree.
The owls hoot with silly rhymes,
While shadows juggle limey limes.

A rabbit's hat holds quite a show,
With carrots pulled from deep below.
And if you peek behind the bark,
A raccoon's having quite a lark.

So join the dance, forget your woes,
The forest knows how laughter flows.
With whimsy wrapped in leafy charms,
Come share the joy that nature farms.

Melodies of a Leafy Realm

In a leafy realm, where shadows play tricks,
A chameleon croons, trying to fix.
He said with a chuckle, 'Is this my new hue?
I blend with the air; can you see me too?'

With a gust of wind, a gust of glee,
Fluffy clouds joined, oh so carefree.
A concert of chirps, and giggles galore,
'This leafy party? I want ten more!'

Spirited Paths of Adventure

Through bushes we dart, a wild little chase,
With chipmunks and squirrels joining the race.
We trip over roots, then laugh at our fall,
In the forest we've found, we conquer it all.

A hat on a branch, it waves like a flag,
It beckons us forth, oh, what a good brag!
We dance with the shadows, twirl with delight,
In this silly chaos, everything feels right.

We spot a strange mushroom, like a tiny old man,
Pretending to sleep, like it's part of the plan.
We giggle and wonder what dreams might reside,
In the worlds of the fungi, where secrets abide.

And so we shall wander, with laughter our guide,
Creating great tales, with friends by our side.
Every twist of the trail, another jest to embrace,
In this spirited journey, we'll never lose pace.

The Richness of Wilderness

Oh, the treasures we find in each leafy nook,
A squirrel with style, in its grand little crook.
It's sporting a nut, like a shiny gold prize,
While we stifle our laughter and roll our wide eyes.

The trees wear their cloaks, so majestically green,
They rustle and whisper, with secrets unseen.
We ask for directions, but the leaves just shake,
As if they are laughing, a big leafy fake.

Raccoons plot mischief, their eyes all aglow,
They offer us snacks—oh, where did they go?
Chasing our footsteps, a hilarious scene,
In this comedic play where nature's the queen.

So here we find joy in unexpected places,
With laughter and fun, in the wild's warm embraces.
The richness we gather is laughter and cheer,
In the wilderness bountiful, we hold it all dear.

Tales of Tranquility

In the calm of the glade, where the whispers resound,
A frog holds a meeting, where creatures abound.
With a tie made of reeds, it jumps up to speak,
While crickets compose a symphonic tweak.

A turtle in glasses is taking a nap,
Dreaming of races, or perhaps a mishap.
We chuckle at nature's delightful array,
In the midst of the calmness, hilarity's play.

Clouds drift above, playing hide and seek,
As shadows trip lightly on the soft creek.
We sit back and watch, under skies so grand,
With giggles and grins, the whole world feels planned.

In this serenity, laughter takes flight,
Painting the quiet with joy and delight.
These tales that we weave in tranquility's throng,
Are filled with the laughter that carries us along.

The Resilient Embrace

In the garden, blooms dance high,
A bee in a suit, a tiny spy.
Chasing petals, in dizzy whirls,
Nature giggles, as chaos unfurls.

Sipping nectar, the squirrel takes flight,
Wearing acorns, oh what a sight!
Robin sings jokes, so offbeat and loud,
Leaves join the laughter, a joyful crowd.

As flowers tumble, and daisies peek,
A hedgehog snickers, with quills so chic.
The sun winks bright, in playful decree,
Nature's comedy, wild and free.

Under the moon, a fox starts to prance,
With bunny pals, they all join the dance.
Whispers of mirth float through the night,
In this merry tale, all feels just right.

Fables of Folklore

Once in a meadow, cows wore shades,
Telling tall tales, in sun's parade.
A sheep in a beret, a goat on a flute,
Mirthful legends, played out in salute.

The owl, the sage, with spectacles round,
Pondered life's jokes as wisdom unbound.
While the turtles waddled, slow with a grin,
Playing tag with the breeze, in their shell-sporting skin.

Frogs croaked sonnets, on lily pad thrones,
Under stars twinkling like playful stones.
A stork flew by, with a hat too big,
Whispering secrets, doing a jig.

In this wild world of whimsy and cheer,
Every creature feels welcome, my dear.
So gather the laughter, let stories unfold,
For here in the fields, life's treasures are gold.

The Heartbeat of Nature

In the woods, a rabbit tells jokes,
With squirrels keen, and nutty folks.
They chuckle loud, 'til branches shake,
The trees lean in, for nature's sake.

A chorus of crickets, a rhythmic delight,
Tap dancing shadows, under moonlight.
While a bear in a tutu takes center stage,
With a twirl and a growl, he's quite the sage.

The wind, a storyteller, whispering soft,
Makes flowers giggle as they sway aloft.
Each gust's a punchline, a tickle, a tease,
Nature's heartbeat, a laughter that frees.

So join the parade, let joy take its turn,
In this funny realm where wild things yearn.
From valleys to peaks, let the revelry flow,
In nature's embrace, we find joy's glow!

Muses of the Mountain Trail

Up in the hills, where knee-highs run,
A whimsical world beneath the sun.
Chipmunks chatter in clever disguise,
As mountains chuckle, it's no surprise.

A porcupine prances, with style so dapper,
In a feather boa, he's quite the rapper.
With jokes about rocks and clouds that wear frowns,
Each step on the trail, a laugh that astounds.

The wind plays tricks with the leaves on the ground,
In a game of tag that knows no bound.
Each boulder a stage, where creatures perform,
Nature's jesters, breaking the norm.

As sunsets paint stories, in hues bright and bold,
The mountains hum tales, of laughter retold.
So dance with the critters, let mirth be your veil,
On this joyful journey, down the mountain trail.

Celebration of Nature's Bounty

In the garden, veggies dance,
Carrots wear a leafy pants.
Tomatoes giggle, round and bright,
They shine like stars in evening light.

Beets in hats, waving hello,
Zucchinis taking center show.
Corn pops up with a sudden cheer,
Laughter echoes far and near.

Herbs are shaking, feeling bold,
Thyme and basil, stories told.
With every sprout and every sprig,
Nature's humor brings a gig.

So raise a glass to every root,
Let's toast the squash in their cute suit.
A merry feast, let's join the jest,
In nature's bounty, we are blessed.

Laughter Amongst the Leaves

Squirrels chatter, what a scene,
Chasing sunlight, feeling keen.
Birds crack jokes on a tree branch high,
While butterflies flirt and flutter by.

Leaves rustle, sharing the tease,
Whispers of wind, drifting with ease.
A chipmunk slips on dewy grass,
It looks around, hope none will pass.

Mushrooms grinning, round and plump,
With secret tales from every bump.
Nature's giggles, light and free,
Brings a smile for you and me.

So let's dance with twirling vines,
Join the jests of playful pines.
In every rustle, laugh, and cheer,
Nature's humor is always near.

Camouflage of the Hidden Glade

In the glade, things hide and seek,
Where shadows play and crickets speak.
A lizard laughs as it blends in,
In the greenery, it wears a grin.

Mossy rocks chuckle and grin,
While rabbits hop and dive right in.
A wise old owl with feathers sleek,
Offers jokes in wisdom's peak.

Frogs croak jokes in joyful rhymes,
Counting leaves and passing times.
The flowers blush, so bright they sway,
Caught in laughter throughout the day.

In this glade of playful guise,
Nature's sense of humor lies.
Amongst the leaves and hidden trails,
Joyfully, adventure never fails.

Tales from the Twisted Trunks

Twisted trunks have stories told,
Of windy nights and tales of bold.
Trees wear hats crafted by crows,
Each branch whispers as evening glows.

Beneath the bark, a raccoon grins,
He hosts a party, let's begin!
With acorns bouncing, fun and shy,
Filling laughter 'neath the sky.

Knotty roots feel the silly breeze,
Bouncing jokes like bouncing peas.
Sap drips down like gooey glee,
Nature's fun, wild and free.

So gather round, hear the knots,
With each giggle, let's tie our thoughts.
In twisted tales and cheerful songs,
Nature's laughter where all belong.

Resilience Wrapped in Needles

In a forest so bright and green,
A tiny shrub with a spiky sheen.
It laughs at storms that come and go,
Wrapped in armor, stealing the show.

The squirrels think it's all a joke,
They use it as a trampoline poke.
While nature's children dance in glee,
This prickly plant sips its tea.

With needles sharp and a touch of flair,
It winks at the sun, without a care.
"Who needs a hug?" it seems to say,
"I prefer a tickle, come what may!"

So when you see it standing tall,
Remember it's here to laugh, not fall.
In the wild, it's truly divine,
A jester cloaked in nature's design.

Spirit of the Mountain's Heart

Atop the peaks, where eagles fly,
A sprightly shrub waves at the sky.
With roots that dance in rocky beds,
It jokes with clouds, nods to its threads.

Like a mountain goat with high-flying dreams,
This sturdy plant bursts at the seams.
It laughs at gravity as it climbs,
In harmony with nature's rhymes.

Local squirrels have deemed it wise,
"Join us for fun!" they chirp and rise.
The shrub replies with a sassy grin,
"Only if you promise to let me win!"

Through snow and hail, it never pouts,
Just chuckles along while the wind shouts.
With every quirk, it shines so bright,
The spirit of mountains, a pure delight.

Aroma of the Emerald Canopy

Under leaves of emerald green,
A mischievous aroma is seen.
It whispers secrets to the breeze,
Tickles the noses of buzzing bees.

The forest party's all aglow,
Dancing around, putting on a show.
"Come smell this!" the dandelions tease,
As scents mingle and swirl with ease.

The creatures of dusk break into song,
While fragrance drifts, where it belongs.
"Who stirred the pot?" the raccoon sly,
"Must be that shrub under the sky!"

Laughter erupts at nature's feast,
As aromas play their cheeky beast.
And in this wonder, all agree,
Nature's humor is wild and free.

Light through the Verdant Veil

In a thicket where shadows play,
Sunbeams poke through in a joyful way.
The plants all giggle as light beams in,
Nature's canvas, where fun begins.

A glen of glee, all aglow,
Those beams of sunshine come and go.
"Dodge me, tease me!" the ferns exclaim,
While the willow whispers, "What a game!"

Now butterflies swoop and sway,
Playing hide-and-seek throughout the day.
"Who will find me? I'm hard to see!"
And blushing blooms join the spree.

Through this veil of verdant cheer,
The budding laughter draws us near.
In this splendor, we all rejoice,
In nature's heart, we find our voice.

An Ode to the Thicket

In a garden where the green leaves wave,
A squirrel prances, bold and brave.
He pauses, stares at a buzzing bee,
Then runs like mad—oh, what glee!

With branches bent in playful sway,
The thicket giggles throughout the day.
A rabbit hops with a jaunty flair,
Dances with shadows, without a care.

Beneath the sun, the shadows play,
A whispering breeze sweeps leaves away.
A frog sings loud from his lily pad,
While joinin' in fun, the turtle's glad.

A fox gets dizzy, chasing his tail,
As birds join in with a chirpy wail.
Together they frolic, a whimsical lot,
In the heart of the thicket, joy is caught.

Embrace of the Evergreen

In the forest, tall and grand,
Pines stretch out their joyful hands.
A raccoon peeks from behind a tree,
He finds a snack and shouts, "Woohoo! Me!"

Around the trunks, the laughter soars,
As branches sway and nature roars.
Squirrels exchange their nutty dreams,
While the sunlight dances in playful beams.

With every turn, a surprise awaits,
A friendly bear who steals the plates.
"Dinner's ready!" the owl hoots loud,
While chipmunks giggle, feeling proud.

In this home of green delights,
Joy is simple; it takes its flights.
With every inch of space we trot,
Each silly moment—oh, it's hot!

Calm in the Qualm

When worries creep like sneaky weeds,
The trees whisper their gentle creeds.
A good-natured breeze sways all around,
Turning frowns into giggles sound.

On a branch, a parrot squawks with zest,
Declaring loudly, "I'm quite the best!"
A skunk rolls by in a flashy stance,
Showing off in a dapper dance.

As clouds play peek-a-boo in the sky,
A lone raccoon gives a playful sigh.
"Oh, the world's too big to take it all,"
He chuckles softly, then starts to fall.

With each mishap, the laughter grows,
In this wonderland of silly prose.
A day spent here feels light and free,
Calm in the chaos, oh, what a spree!

Sips of Nature's Nectar

In the meadow's patch, a picnic spread,
A playful bear finds cake instead.
With frosting smeared upon his snout,
He dances 'round, without a doubt.

Upon a branch, a party starts,
With ladybugs and tiny tarts.
The ants march in with their tiny treats,
Twirling in rhythm to nature's beats.

A bumblebee buzzes, sipping nectar sweet,
While butterflies twirl, oh, what a feat!
Their colorful wings against the sun,
Joining in laughter, they play and run.

When day turns dusk, the stars appear,
Nature's nectar flows, spreading cheer.
Each critter winks in this joyous scene,
Celebrating life, forever keen.

Mysteries of the Shadowed Glen

In the glen where shadows dance,
A squirrel steals a tomato, not by chance.
The owls hoot, full of surprise,
As rabbits plot under darkened skies.

The ferns giggle, tickled by the breeze,
While crickets ask if they can freeze.
A deer sneezes, causing quite a stir,
As a hedgehog whispers, "That's not ajar!"

Fluffy clouds look down and grin,
Watching chaos as creatures spin.
The groundhog snorts, can't find its way,
In twisted paths where pranks hold sway.

Oh, the secrets that nature will weave,
In laughter's embrace, we all believe.
Unraveling jest beneath the trees,
In the glen's wild heart, we all find ease.

Places Where the Wild Things Sing

Where wild things gather, tunes abound,
In wacky corners of the ground.
A frog croaks out a jazz man's beat,
While fireflies shimmer, dancing on feet.

A bear hums closely, off-key yet bold,
As raccoons share tales, both funny and old.
The hedgehogs clap with tiny hands,
Cheering for critters in funky bands.

Among the bushes, laughter erupts,
With dancing shadows, the night disrupts.
A rabbit jigs in wild delight,
As owls spin tunes in the pale moonlight.

Oh, sing the melodies that lift us high,
Where wild things laugh, and spirits fly.
In raucous joy, the night will sway,
In these places, we'll laugh and play.

The Spirit of the Underbrush

In the underbrush where the wild things roam,
A lizard claims it's found a home.
Mice chatter with glee about snacks galore,
While critters try to settle old scores!

A fox plays tricks with a twitch of its tail,
Teasing the rabbit, "You'll never prevail!"
The beetles race in a tireless spree,
While ants humor them with their tiny glee.

The mushrooms wiggle, giggling aloud,
As shadows play tricks, so mischief is proud.
The thorns and vines conspire to poke,
While cacti snicker with every joke.

Oh, the antics that thrive in low lands,
In the underbrush, we make our plans.
With laughter bubbling, joy fills the air,
Where the spirit of mirth is beyond compare.

Timeless Tales of the Timberland

In the timberland, stories take flight,
With each twist of the branches, a new delight.
A pine tree whispers secrets so sly,
As morning doves share a giggly sigh.

The berries hold meetings, plotting their scheme,
While raccoons discuss their next daring dream.
The owls watch closely, wise yet bemused,
At antics clever and often confused.

Squirrels with acorns, ready to launch,
Creating chaos—a nut-filled haunch!
While moss giggles under mischievous feet,
The tales of the forest will never be beat.

So let's toast to these moments we find,
In the timberland's heart, where laughter is kind.
With timeless tales wrapped in nature's delight,
Where fun and frolic brighten the night.

Rhythms of the Wild

In the forest, dances abound,
Squirrels twirl, all around.
Branches sway without a care,
Birds hum tunes, a lively flair.

Mossy carpets, soft and grand,
Tickle toes, oh isn't it bland?
Nature's rhythm, a silly beat, `
With every bounce, they tap their feet.

Frogs debate the best of flies,
While ants march on, in a line that ties.
A raccoon juggles acorns high,
And laughter echoes, oh me, oh my!

Nature's party, come take a peep,
Where even the trees giggle and leap.

A Breath of Mossy Air

In the woods, a breath so sweet,
Mossy scents, can't be beat.
Raccoons mime with clever grace,
While chipmunks stash, their cheeks embrace.

Wicked winds, they tease and play,
Turning leaves in a funny sway.
Nature whispers silly pranks,
In this home of leafy banks.

Lizards lounge, in sun they bake,
Proclaiming themselves, a true mistake.
But here we laugh, no need to care,
For every joke hangs in the air.

With every breath, a giggle squeaks,
Mossy whispers fill the weeks.

Trails of Ancient Wisdom

Among the trees, old sages chat,
Teaching wise ways, in the format of a hat.
'Tis the ant who rules the line,
With comical tales of gardens divine.

The owls wink, and hoot with glee,
Dropping jokes from every tree.
Cacophony of chuckles clear,
Ancient wisdom, far from drear.

The wise old tree shares tales so vast,
Of squirrels lost and shadows cast.
Every leaf, a scripted joke,
In the breeze, their laughter woke.

Paths of humor, winding away,
In the woods, we laugh and play.

Secrets Amongst the Branches

In the boughs, secrets align,
Bees gossip like they're sipping wine.
Branches chat, with leaves so bright,
Whispering tales until the night.

Feathered friends, they sing on cue,
As if rehearsed for me and you.
Each flutter brings a tale that spins,
Of silly bugs and impish grins.

Woodpeckers tap in a silly tune,
While mushrooms giggle under the moon.
A race of critters, quicken their pace,
In this woods' great, funny space.

Secrets flutter, laughter's call,
Amongst the branches, we share it all.

Nature's Whispered Lullaby

In the forest where squirrels dance,
Chasing shadows with every chance.
A raccoon wearing a tiny hat,
Winks at you, then scurries flat.

Breezes carry giggles and sighs,
Leaves are laughing, oh what a surprise.
A wise old owl gives a soft hoot,
"Don't mind the deer in those bright red boots!"

Frogs in tuxedos leap with flair,
To serenade the sweet, cool air.
A rabbit juggles acorns with glee,
"Come join my show, it's just for free!"

So lie beneath this starry quilt,
Nature's humor, never felt.
Let the laughter of woods unfold,
In this carnival, life is gold.

Twilit Trails of Wonder

Strolling down paths where shadows play,
Fireflies twinkle, come join their ballet.
A fox with glasses reads a book,
"Beware of rocks!" as he gives a look.

Crickets chirp their secret song,
While a turtle claims he's running strong.
"Just watch me, friends!" he calls with zest,
But he's still napping, like all the rest.

The moon grins wide, a jovial face,
Lighting up this delightful place.
Opossum stumbles, then takes a bow,
Dreams of acorns, oh where, oh how?

Nature giggles beneath the stars,
Mischief dances, in tangle of bars.
Once more onward, our laughter sway,
On twilit trails, let's frolic and play!

Secrets of the Verdant Path

Whispers emerge from the mossy ground,
Where curious critters can always be found.
A hedgehog in sandals takes a stroll,
"Life's too short to not rock and roll!"

Mushrooms all gather for tea at dusk,
Sipping dew drops, in nature we trust.
A skunk jokes, "I've got a real nice scent,
But only if you pay my rent!"

Winding pathways weave tales untold,
Where even the shyest creatures grow bold.
A snail shouts, "I'm fast, I promise you!
Just give me a minute, or maybe two!"

The sun bids farewell with a naughty wink,
As critters linger, they laugh and think.
Secrets abound, as the moon's light starts,
Nature's laughter dances within our hearts.

The Enchanted Grove

In the grove where laughter springs,
Trees tell tales of wondrous things.
A gnome tells jokes to a wilting flower,
"Ever tried dance in this twilight hour?"

Bunnies bounce in mismatched socks,
Dodging toads who play checkers on rocks.
A sparrow chirps with comedic flair,
"Why did the worm go up in the air?"

Echoes of mirth through the branches soar,
Every critter joins, asking for more.
The moon starts to chuckle, its glow so bright,
"Let's party till dawn, it's pure delight!"

In this enchanted grove, joy abounds,
Even the crickets dance with sounds.
Nature revels in whimsical show,
Brightening hearts wherever you go.

Facets of Forest Light

In the woods where shadows play,
A squirrel thinks it owns the day.
With acorns stashed in pockets tight,
It dances in the dappled light.

A rabbit hops on thumping feet,
Chasing dreams of veggies sweet.
But slips on moss—a comical sight,
'This forest's quite a tricky flight!'

A chipmunk hums a tune off-key,
While bees invade a bumblebee.
In tangled roots, they twist and twine,
Behold the antics, oh divine!

The trees above do creak and sway,
As nature laughs throughout the day.
With each rustle and swish of leaf,
The forest tells a tale of grief.

Hues of the Heartwood

A woodpecker's drum is loud, you see,
While tree frogs croak in harmony.
They've formed a band in vibrant hues,
But have no clue how much they bruise.

A porcupine struts, feeling grand,
With quills that sparkle, oh so planned.
Yet, when it tries to dance a jig,
It fumbles—oh, that's quite the gig!

A fox appears with swagger bright,
Proud of its fur, a glorious sight.
But trips on roots with a yelp and squeal,
"I swear I didn't eat that meal!"

The laughter echoes far and wide,
Among the trees where critters hide.
In this wild mix of fun and frolic,
Nature scripts the tales symbolic.

Reverberations Among the Greenery

Branches clatter in breezy cheer,
As whispers circulating appear.
"Did you hear? The owl's gone bold,
   Singing karaoke for a gold!"

A badger grins, its eyes so bright,
When it stumbles upon a fright.
It rolls in mud, a muddled mess,
Then strikes a pose—what confidence!

As laughter ripples through the leaves,
A web of giggles the forest weaves.
A family of deer plays peek-a-boo,
   "Catch us if you can!" they coo.

On every path, where silliness roams,
The earth becomes their laughter's home.
With fables spun in bright moonlight,
   This greenery brings sheer delight.

Lush Fields and Ferns

In fields so green, the daisies sway,
While butterflies debate their way.
"Do we go left? Or take the right?"
They flit and flutter, quite a flight!

Ferns rise up to share their tale,
Of a snail's race, slow but pale.
"I'm winning!" it shouts with glee,
While pals just laugh, "You're out, you see?"

A hedgehog rolls, a tiny ball,
What a scene—oh what a brawl!
With friends who tumble, spin and dive,
They play all day, so much alive!

Through fields of green, the laughter rolls,
Nature's heartbeat, filling souls.
In every nook, a jest to share,
Amidst the blooms, joy fills the air.

Serene Sylvan Secrets

In the forest, whispers giggle,
Squirrels plotting their next wiggle.
Trees wear hats made of leafy glee,
Nature's jesters, wild and free.

Mice in tuxedos dance on logs,
Debating life with the moonlit frogs.
Fungi throw a party, quite the sight,
With toadstools as chairs, oh what a night!

Beneath the branches, laughter rings,
A ladybug queen, on her throne she sings.
Rabbits play cards, rather sly,
While owls hoot at clouds passing by.

So next time you roam the woods anew,
Remember the secrets that trees construe.
For nature's humor is a wondrous show,
Wait, did that bush just wink? Oh no!

Evergreen Elegance

Pinecone crowns on headless trees,
Nature's fashion, a breeze through leaves.
Squirrels strut like they own the place,
With nutty flair, and nibbled grace.

The stream giggles, bubbling with glee,
Rocks play leapfrog, oh can't you see?
Fluffy clouds drift with dreamy laughs,
While turtles debate, who has the fastest paths?

Birds with sass chirp cheeky tunes,
While dandelions dance to beneath the moons.
In the boughs above, mischief unfurls,
As ants throw a rave, oh what twirling swirls!

So wander a path lined with delight,
Join nature's ballet, a true feathered flight.
For in green realms, laughter may grow,
Just watch your step; it's a slippery show!

Aromas of the Forest

Mossy carpets with scents divine,
Where pine and laughter twist and twine.
Bears don hats for a gourmet meal,
Raccoons trade cookies, it's a big deal!

Crisp leaves crunch like popcorn gold,
Trees gossip tales of the brave and bold.
Bumblebees with fancies aflutter,
Dream of finding the best peanut butter.

Frogs croon songs from their hidden pond,
While fireflies twinkle, a dance to respond.
Underneath the ferns, secrets unfold,
Nature's whispers, tales never told.

So step into this fragrant spree,
Where woodland wonders play just for thee.
In the heart of green, let giggles bloom,
As aromas of joy send away your gloom!

Beneath the Canopy's Embrace

Beneath the trees, shadows play tricks,
Branches waving like those at a fix.
A wiggle-legged crab makes a grand speech,
While butterflies float just out of reach.

Kittens in the underbrush plot a surprise,
Trading secrets with owls that wise.
The sun tickles leaves with a golden grin,
As frogs in tuxedos prepare for a spin.

Bark beetles laugh, the humor is thick,
As acorns improvise, quick thinking their trick.
Dancing in circles, the critters rejoice,
For nature's a stage, and this is their choice.

So, if wandering here strikes your fancy,
Join this woodland party, oh so chancy.
For beneath this bough, let merriment chase,
A funny little world, in this wild space!

Songs of Soft Shadows

In a corner of the park, where shadows play,
The squirrels dance in hats, all of them sway.
With acorns held high, they lift up a cheer,
For the world's a grand stage, let joy persevere.

The butterflies join, in polka-dot hats,
While the bunnies tap dance, with pitter-pat pats.
Each leaf in the breeze becomes part of the fun,
As laughter erupts under the warm, golden sun.

The trees sway in rhythm, a natural band,
And the ants form a line, marching so grand.
With each silly step, the frogs croak along,
Creating a chorus, a whimsical song.

So, gather your friends, let's join this parade,
In shadows and silliness, there's no need for trade.
For joy is contagious, it'll spread like a flood,
In the park's soft embraces, we dance in the mud.

Secrets of the Shadow Realm

In the shadows they whisper, secrets untold,
Where gnomes tell tall tales, and mischief unfolds.
With winks and with giggles, conspiracies bloom,
As the flowers roll over to hide from the gloom.

A dragon sneezes, and smoke fills the air,
While fairies in capes fly without a care.
They trip on their wings, tumble, laugh, and roll,
In this realm of shadows, they find their own soul.

The owls play poker, bluffing their foes,
With rabbits as dealers and all in their clothes.
The stakes are quite high, just a carrot or two,
Yet the laughter is louder than any old clue.

If you venture this way, keep your sense of fun,
For in this shadow realm, there's nowhere to run.
The giggles are endless, the joy like a dream,
In the heart of the dark, where nothing's as it seems.

The Charm of Hidden Groves

Deep in the woods, where mischief hides,
There's a grove full of laughter, where silliness resides.
The trees wear their best, with leaves all askew,
As they tickle the clouds in a whimsical brew.

Beneath every rock, a secret is found,
A frog with a top hat, leaping around.
He croaks crooning tunes to the critters that cheer,
With a wink and a nod, spreading joy far and near.

The hedgehogs are jamming, with berries for drums,
And turtles do the limbo, while the raccoon hums.
Each corner's a party, an unexpected spree,
In this hidden grove, wild and fancy-free.

So pack up your giggles, don't leave them behind,
To the groves full of charm, where the world's so kind.
Under branches of laughter, you'll surely rejoice,
For the magic is real; it's a giggler's choice.

A Saga of Serenity

In the land of calm where the breeze sways slow,
A cow doesn't moo, instead shares a flow.
With sheep on guitars and chickens in hats,
Serenity sings with all of her chats.

The sun winks down on meadows so wide,
While goats in their sweaters take us for a ride.
They dance like they're crazy, jumping around,
As they lace up their boots in a hilarious bound.

Clouds play peek-a-boo with the soft, gentle pines,
While rabbits compose their own silly rhymes.
Each whisper they share carries joy in the air,
In this saga of peace, where nothing's unfair.

So wander with laughter through fields of delight,
Where the joyous and funny unite in pure light.
For the saga is written in giggles and grins,
In a world where serenity truly begins.

Beneath the Elder Trees

Under branches wide, we prance,
Chasing shadows, goofing by chance.
Squirrels laugh at our silly games,
While we shout out each other's names.

The mushrooms giggle as we trip,
One by one, we start to slip.
Nature's stage, our grand ballet,
Dancing wildly, come what may.

With elder trees, our friends so dear,
We chuckle loud, we share our cheer.
The breeze just winks, it knows our plans,
To twirl and leap in silly stances.

As the sun sets, we strike a pose,
A snapshot caught, our friendship glows.
Underneath the elder trees,
A joy so wild, carried on the breeze.

A Story of Growth

In a garden small, we find our fate,
Dandelions burst, we celebrate.
With laughter loud, we plant our seeds,
While telling tales of daring deeds.

A worm in a hat joins our parade,
Tickling our feet, he plans his trade.
Selling dreams for a slice of pie,
We giggle hard, oh me, oh my!

The daisies wink, the roses grin,
As we recount our wildest win.
Each sprout a story, each leaf a laugh,
We'll grow together on this path.

Sunflowers tall, with heads held high,
Try to dance, but just end up shy.
Yet every bloom, a funny tale,
In this patch, you'll never fail!

The Palette of Earth's Palette

Colors clash where we walk today,
Pinks and greens in a vibrant display.
A rainbow fight with paint-stained hands,
Each splash of color, wild demands.

Grass stains and laughter, we cannot hide,
A mess of hues, we wear with pride.
The sunbeams laugh, they shine brighter still,
As we roll down the soft green hill.

With every hue, a story unfolds,
Of pranks and playful, daring golds.
Our joyous mess, the artist's dream,
We're painting joy, or so it seems.

At day's end, with colors all askew,
We sit and ponder what more to do.
With paint on our cheeks, we nod in glee,
Nature's palette, the best of a spree!

Whispers of the Wind

The wind whispers secrets, soft and sly,
Like a mischievous sprite passing by.
It tickles our ears with silly tunes,
And carries our laughter to the moons.

Through fields we race, a carefree flight,
While dandelion seeds take joyful height.
We catch them all, like giggles in jars,
Releasing them gently, like wishes on stars.

Branches sway, with a gentle caress,
The wind hides treasures in its mess.
We listen close for the mischief it sows,
As it dances among the blooming rows.

With each gust, we shout out a cheer,
For the playful breeze, our friend so dear.
Together we frolic, in nature's grand spin,
Whispers of the wind, let the fun begin!

Tapestry of Twisted Branches

In a garden where all branches twist,
The squirrels dance, you can't resist.
One's in a hat, another in shoes,
Nature's circus, oh, what a muse!

A crow's got a goal, oh what a play,
Stealing my lunch every single day.
With each little heist, it caws with glee,
I swear it knows it's ruining me!

A hedgehog prances like it's a star,
Dreaming of fame like it's seen from afar.
But rolls it keeps, like a furry ball,
Who needs a spotlight when you're this small?

So I laugh and I giggle, can't help but share,
This tangled life, it's beyond compare.
In my twisted garden, where laughter blooms,
Every little critter finds joy in their rooms.

Hues of Earth and Sky

The sky wore blue, the ground was brown,
A chicken strutted, king of the town.
With every cluck, it claimed the day,
Twirling in dust, in its own ballet!

A rabbit hopped, with a wink and a grin,
Trying to catch that chicken's spin.
Round and round like a dizzy dream,
Their antics spark laughter, or so it seems!

A turtle slow, waving high while it passed,
Shouted, "You kids, will you hurry up fast?"
But they kept spinning in rhythmic delight,
A fun little chaos, what a sight!

Colors collided as the sun took a dive,
Nature's laughter made everything come alive.
In hues of joy, under the sprawling sky,
Every living creature took a moment to fly.

The Solstice Sprout

A sprout decided it was time to grow,
It poked its head from the earth below.
But tripped on worms, what a silly scene,
Grumbling and mumbling, feeling quite mean!

A ladybug giggled, rolling with cheer,
"Get up, sprout! The sun is near!"
And off it went like a speedy dash,
Chasing the light, with a joyful splash!

But then a rain cloud felt a little shy,
And drizzled drops from up in the sky.
The sprout had fun, though it got a bit wet,
Dancing in puddles without a regret!

Soon all the plants joined the sprout in glee,
When sun came out, oh what jubilee!
A solstice party, nature's delight,
With laughter and growth, from morning to night.

Echoes in the Evergreen Grove

In the grove where whispers twist and turn,
A pinecone dropped with a little churn.
"Look out below!" it shouted in glee,
Landing on a squirrel, hiding with tea!

The branches giggle with a leafy cheer,
As acorns tumble, it's a grand frontier.
But here comes a deer, trying to blend,
With leaves on its head, oh, what a trend!

A raccoon watched, giving a sly wink,
"Fashion's a game, don't forget to think!"
Wobbling like it had too much to eat,
Chasing the shadows on nimble feet.

In whispers and laughter, the grove would sing,
A symphony of nature, let the fun spring!
With echoes of joy, in the emerald mist,
Every creature living can't help but persist.

Harmony in the Hedges

In a garden green, a squirrel prances,
Chasing shadows, taking chances.
With acorns flying, it starts to twirl,
Oh, what a show, such a merry whirl!

Birds chirp loud, a raucous tune,
As crickets leap beneath the moon.
Each leaf a stage for a comical play,
Nature's antics brighten the day.

Tiny bugs in a grand parade,
Wearing uniforms of klutzy jade.
With each misstep and clumsy pose,
Laughter erupts from every rose.

In this hedge, the laughter grows,
Nature's jesters and their prose.
So come and share this quirky glee,
Where every critter is wild and free.

Petals of Time

Upon the breeze, petals giggle,
As time passes, they dance and wiggle.
In a mess of colors, they blend with cheer,
Each fallen bloom whispers, 'We're here!'

The bees buzz in a bustling line,
While ants confuse the sun for wine.
They march in circles—where to go?
In this funny world, we steal the show!

Time plays tricks, as it tends to do,
With seconds that fly and minutes askew.
A flower yawns, then sneezes—achoo!
And the petals laugh, 'Oh, how rude of you!'

With every tick, the petals jive,
In this playful dance, we all feel alive.
So gather round, let mirth refine,
In the garden of giggles, we'll watch time shine!

Raindrops on Evergreen Needles

Raindrops tumble, giggling loud,
Sliding down, beneath a cloud.
Each one lands with a splish and splash,
Creating puddles in a joyful dash.

Evergreen needles wear a smile,
Dancing droplets make it worthwhile.
With a wink and a wet little cheer,
They invite all creatures, drawing near.

A frog leaps out from his leafy throne,
With a croak that dances like a cheerful drone.
While worms wiggle in their muddy ballet,
In this rainy shindig, they all want to play!

The air is fresh, the world's alive,
In this wet wonderland, we thrive.
So let's rejoice, let's sing and glide,
In drops of laughter, let joy abide.

Boughs of Bliss

Boughs sway gently, beneath the breeze,
Whispering secrets among the trees.
They tickle the sky, as they bend and twist,
Inviting the world to join their tryst.

Squirrels chatter, with sneakers on paws,
Playing tag without a pause.
Their antics send giggles to the ground,
In this canopy, where fun is found.

Sunlight peeks through, a mischievous grin,
Filling the forest with light within.
The branches chuckle, a delightful sound,
In this joyful ruckus, true bliss is found.

So let us romp, let us play near,
With laughter and cheer, year after year.
Underneath the boughs, let worries dismiss,
In this whimsical world, we find pure bliss.

Roots of Happiness in the Earth

Beneath the ground, worms have a ball,
They wiggle and squirm, never feel small.
Dancing in soil, with radishes bright,
Laughing at veggies, what a delight!

The beetroot wears boots, it likes to parade,
While carrots wear hats, oh what a charade!
Earth giggles softly, in patches of green,
With roots in their pockets, the best of the scene!

Flowers are gossiping, oh what a sight,
Sipping on sunshine, feeling just right.
The daisies and roses share tales from the sun,
Who knew being happy could be so much fun?

While moles dig their tunnels, they trip on a stone,
Stumbling and laughing as they whine and moan.
With roots twirling gently, a dance underground,
The party in earth is the best to be found!

The Colors of Harmony in Nature

A bluebird sings loudly, it finds it hilarious,
While the green grass chuckles, quite gregarious.
Yellow dandelions join in the fun,
Tickling the breeze, they're second to none!

The sky wears a smile, clouds puffy and bright,
While butterflies giggle in a colorful flight.
Red roses tease violets with laughs full of glee,
Nature's palette swings, in sync, full of spree!

A sweet little squirrel, a nut in his grip,
Trips on a twig, does an acrobatic flip.
Laughter erupts from the leaves in the trees,
Who knew harmony could tickle like these?

With laughter like raindrops, a splash in the air,
Colors collide in a joyous affair.
The hues of the world, a canvas of cheer,
Nature's own giggle, oh, how it draws near!

Tranquility Amongst the Branches

A wise old owl, with spectacles neat,
Counts all the stars, then falls asleep.
The squirrels debate how to steal a nut,
While chipmunks giggle, 'You're stuck in a rut!'

Swaying with breezes, the branches sway slow,
Tickling the bark, making it glow.
A gentle breeze whispers jokes to the leaves,
Nature's comedians pulling up their sleeves!

The raccoons at night put on a grand show,
Stealing the snacks, all under one glow.
With laughter and snickers, the forest is bright,
Tranquility thrives when funny's in sight!

As crickets tap dance and fireflies blink,
Branches embrace as the forest winks.
In playful togetherness, life's such a jest,
Amongst all the branches, we find our best!

Soundtrack of the Swaying Pines

Swaying pine trees hum a catchy tune,
Their needles like strings, strumming 'round noon.
A concert of rustles, a melody sweet,
While critters tap dance, shuffling their feet!

The wind picks up tempo, whoosh through the boughs,
Conducting a symphony, taking a bow.
Bouncing acorns roll, keeping the beat,
Nature's orchestra, nothing can compete!

The sunbeams drop in for a solo, you know,
While shadows wiggle, putting on quite a show.
Nature's remix spins, with giggles galore,
A soundtrack of joy that we can't ignore!

With every chorus, the pines stand so tall,
Whispering secrets, inviting us all.
Creating sweet laughter, a song of delight,
In the sway of the pines, everything feels right!

Nature's Canvas in Emerald

In emerald green with sprigs so bright,
Little critters dance with delight.
They paint the air with giggles and glee,
While squirrels play hide and seek with the bees.

A rabbit hops in a polka-dot suit,
Chasing a butterfly in pursuit.
The trees wear hats of mossy delight,
While crows recite poems full of insight.

Dewdrops laugh on blades of grass,
Sharing secrets as they pass.
The sun tickles leaves, a playful tease,
While the wind whispers jokes to the trees.

In this wild canvas, life's a jest,
A place where nature's humor is best.
With every step, a chuckle takes flight,
In a world where silliness feels just right.

A Symphony of Scent

A waft of thyme hits the nose,
As bees in tiny tuxedos pose.
With rosemary hats and parsley flair,
They serenade snails all unaware.

The roses giggle, their colors bright,
Flirting with daisies, oh, what a sight!
A perfume battle on a breezy day,
Where lilies claim they smell better, hip-hip-hooray!

Lavender whispers, "I'm the queen,"
While clover winks, "Don't be so mean!"
Petunias chuckle, "Your scent's too strong!"
As the garden hums its fragrant song.

In this symphony of scents, we find,
Nature's humor, quirky and kind.
With every whiff, a giggle erupts,
In a fragrant world where fun disrupts.

The Shelter of Solitude

Under a tree, I find my peace,
Where whispers of leaves steadily crease.
A squirrel's chatter, a stand-up act,
With jokes about acorns—oh, how they pack!

The mushrooms giggle, wearing their caps,
While crickets drum on their tiny laps.
I sit in silence, but oh, what a show,
As nature's jesters put on a glow.

A lizard does yoga; I can't help but stare,
While ants march by in a quirky pair.
Each moment a laugh, in solitude's hold,
Nature's laughter, a treasure untold.

In this shelter, I chuckle and grin,
Finding joy in the dance of a fin.
Alone, yet surrounded by giggles and cheer,
Nature's humor makes solitude dear.

Twilight Glow in the Glade

As twilight falls, the fireflies blink,
Dancing like stars—oh, what a wink!
The trees start gossiping in secret tones,
While mushrooms gossip on their little thrones.

A raccoon in boots sways to a tune,
Under the enchanting glow of the moon.
He juggles acorns like tiny balls,
While frogs join in with their ribbits and calls.

Crickets play violins, a serenade,
As the evening parade begins in the glade.
The owls hoot jokes, puffed up with pride,
With thoughts of the laughter they just can't hide.

In twilight's charm, the world feels right,
Where creatures of humor come out at night.
And as I sit back to enjoy the show,
Nature's comedy steals the glow.

The Note of Nature's Chorus

In the woods, trees whisper low,
Squirrels dance, putting on a show.
Bouncing branches, a leafy band,
Nature's tunes, perfectly unplanned.

Frogs croak like they own the stage,
While bugs play cards, set the rage.
Bees are buzzing, not a care,
Got honey to share with dreams in the air.

The sun beams down, a golden grin,
While rabbits join in, 'Let the fun begin!'
A chorus of laughter fills the breeze,
Nature's humor, an infectious tease.

In the woods, we find our rhyme,
Every moment, a jest in time.
So join the fun, don't be late,
For nature's laughter is truly great.

Garden of Stone and Sprout

In the garden where veggies dwell,
Tomatoes gossip, got tales to tell.
Carrots chuckle, peeking out green,
'What's life without a little bean?'

Gnomes wear hats that wobble and sway,
They join the veggies in their display.
Stone-faced, yet giggles abound,
In this wee patch, wonders are found.

Weeds waltz in, crashing the tea,
'Thought you'd forget us, oh can't you see?'
Lettuce rolls, on the soft ground they crash,
While radishes blush with a rosy flash.

So come and laugh at nature's array,
In this garden, let joy lead the way.
With every sprout, and every laugh,
Life's a dance and nature's the path.

Memories Stitched in Green

At dawn, the grass wears dewdrops bright,
A canvas of memories, pure delight.
Dandelions giggle as children run,
Every stitch in green, a memory spun.

Whimsical clouds float, puffy and grand,
Recollecting moments, joys unplanned.
The sun releases a playful shout,
'Let nostalgia dance and twirl about!'

Snakes in the grass play hide and seek,
While crickets serenade with a cheeky squeak.
Through laughter, through sighs, we trace our days,
Nature's embrace, a whimsical maze.

So raise a toast to each memory made,
In the tapestry of green, we wade.
With each bough and brook, joy is seen,
In stories stitched, our moments glean.

Breath of the Wooded Realm

In the woods where giggles roam free,
The trees clap hands, just wait and see.
A squirrel stumbles, gives a cheer,
'Nature's a laugh, let's spread the cheer!'

Mushrooms grin in their polka dot suits,
While hedgehogs hide in their spiky boots.
The air is thick with playful scents,
As nature plots its prankish events.

Owl hoots jokes from his hollowed nook,
Each punchline stirs from the shadiest book.
Sticks snap like laughter, crickets sing,
In this realm of whimsy, we're all the king.

So take a breath of this wooded cheer,
Where every chuckle is crystal clear.
Join the banter, let moments flow,
In the woods, there's a comedy show!

Whispers of the Woodland Breeze

In the forest, squirrels prance,
With acorns flying in their dance.
Frogs croak jokes upon the log,
While rabbits giggle with each fog.

Leaves rustle with a secret sound,
As woodland friends gather round.
A chattering bird on a sprightly spree,
Yells, "Who's got the best cup of tea?"

The breeze tickles the floppy ears,
While laughter echoes, less than fears.
All the critters in high glee,
Singing songs of jubilee!

In this funky, playful space,
Nature's laughter finds its place.
With smiles bright and tails held high,
The woodland fables never die!

A Dance of Blue-green Needles

Needles twirl in a quirky show,
As the breeze gives them a gentle blow.
The grasses join in a windy jig,
While insects buzz like a dancing pig.

A chipmunk does a little spin,
And all the trees share a cheeky grin.
They clap their branches, stomp their roots,
As if to join in the silly hoots.

A lizard shimmies across a stone,
Challenging the wind to join its throne.
Nature's revel feels like a tease,
Whirling joy in the gentle breeze.

In every twist and turn they make,
There's laughter woven in each quake.
The woodland's charm, a comedy,
Where merriment thrives, so wild and free!

Secrets Amongst the Boughs

Beneath the branches, whispers rise,
As wily creatures plot their lies.
Squirrels, wise, with nimble feet,
Concoct tales of woodland tweets.

A bear in shades thinks he's sly,
Dreaming up a plane to fly.
With honeyed dreams in a clanking jar,
He hums all day, a fuzzy star.

Porcupines gossip near a pine,
While hedgehogs joke about a vine.
What's the secret to the trees?
Stand tall and dance in the breeze!

So gather round for tales untold,
Of nature's jest, both bright and bold.
For secrets here will never end,
Just giggles shared by every friend!

The Fragrance of Sunlit Shadows

In golden rays, the shadows play,
Where butterflies frolic through the fray.
Petals tease with scents so sweet,
Daring noses to take a seat.

A rabbit remarks, with flair so grand,
"Why chase the sun when you can stand?"
While mice share cheese in shadowed light,
In laughter's hug, they feel just right.

The woodland whispers, "Let's unwind,
And leave our worries far behind."
With giggles wafting in the air,
Each creature grins with such a flare.

In this realm of scent and fun,
The laughter sparkles like the sun.
With every breath, they spread good cheer,
In shadows bright, the joy is clear!

www.ingramcontent.com/pod-product-compliance
Lightning Source LLC
Chambersburg PA
CBHW072141200426
43209CB00051B/237